to Dennis.

Best wishes,

from Michael G.

Straight Up
– No Sugar

Straight Up
– No Sugar

Michael Gannon

To Mam, Dad, Jenny and Eoin
for supporting me
throughout my life and in
memory of Nanny Kitty.

Contents

Foreword

I am Michael's sister, Jenny. I was three years old when Michael was born. I don't remember him coming home from hospital but by all accounts I wasn't really sure if he was a real person or a doll, so I decided to find out one day, shortly after he arrived home, by biting his finger. Oops! He was definitely real, and has been every day of his life.

I've often been asked why I don't mention that Michael has Down syndrome when I talk about him to people. I guess it's because I rarely think of his Down syndrome. In many ways it's irrelevant. It is not who he is. Yes, it is part of him but it doesn't define him. He has always been very much his own person. Michael, himself, has always felt very strongly about wanting to be recognised as Michael, not the boy/man with Down syndrome. He has always had ambition (sometimes above his station in life). He has always had his dreams and the irrefutable belief that they will come true.

He is, and has been, an inspiration to me and to all of us who know him well. He is definitely one of the reasons I became a teacher. He instilled in me the belief that every child has an abundance of talent, a great ability to learn, and a unique and inspiring way of viewing the world. Many simply need us grown-ups to think outside the box to help them reach their full potential.

Michael has battled against people's prejudices. He has ignored people's negative opinions, their 'God love him' attitude and 'Sure isn't he great' ideas. He has proved many doubters wrong with his achievements. Michael has a very strong belief in the message held within this book. He believes that people need to understand what life is like for somebody with Down syndrome. He explains how he wants to be seen and treated by others. He celebrates his achievements in the hope that they will allow others to see the real contribution he makes in life.

If you know somebody with Down syndrome and wonder if they have a valuable contribution to make to their community and people in their life, you will find the undeniable answer here in this book. If you wonder what people with Down syndrome think about their own condition, one person's thoughts are here. Michael's story is a testimony to the great abilities and talents that are within each of us.

Jenny Gannon

Introduction

My name is Michael Gannon and I am thirty years of age. I live in Newbridge, County Kildare, Ireland. I like to read books, listen to music and watch DVDs. I also like taking part in shows and meeting new friends. I am into sports, especially hurling and soccer.

I will tell you why I wrote this book. One reason is that I want the readers to understand what my story is about. I want to explain that I was born with Down syndrome. I want you to look at me right now doing the same things as anyone else and living my life to the full. I want to share my experiences with you, my friends.

Another reason why I wrote this book is because it was something different for me to do, and a challenge. I know you might think this sounds daft. This is my first book, and it was hard to write and took a long time. I hope that when you read *Straight Up, No Sugar* you will get to know me for the person that I am, and how I cope with my life.

When you get a chance to read this book – and I hope you do – you will get my message saying that I have Down syndrome but also that I am just me. That is all you really need to know about me. But there is a lot more.

My message to you is please stop looking at Down syndrome and see people. We are the same as anyone around us. We must live our lives to the full. We must follow our dreams.

Most parents wish that their children did not have Down syndrome when they are born. I want to say to the parents that these are your children. Please look at your own child and see more than Down syndrome. If you do, you will feel very proud when you see all the gifts and talents that we have.

I hope that my message will be very strong and hope that all parents will read this book. I want them to see something very different, something that they have never seen. It is very important to me that I make myself heard. I hope that I will

be the voice of the friends that I have made in my life. I think it is important for everyone to have a say in the world and to stand up for themselves. We should all listen to each other.

In my book there are many pictures of me, my family and friends. Sometimes I feel that I am on my own. Then I look back on the photos of myself as a child as I grew up, and that helps me to look to the future with everyone around me. I had never thought that I would do a book. But this became my challenge and I hope to pass the test for myself and for my family and friends.

Photograph by Deasy Photographic

10

My Life

Sometimes life can be hard. At times things do go wrong and I am disappointed. I think it is very important to remember the good times and let go of the bad times.

I know that I have Down syndrome but that does not stop or defeat me, because in my life I have lots of things going on. I am proud of all the things I can do. I will tell you about some of them later in my book. I know how I feel about myself, and mostly it feels good. I do everything for myself. I look after myself well. I always do. I have great friends and they have been great to be with.

I go out with my friends, and we have a few drinks. Sometimes I feel that I am part of a group that does everything. It makes me very happy to get involved more because I am now getting to know everyone, and they know me.

Friends are important, and have a major impact on you. We all do the things we can do together - things like going on holidays together and going to see matches. I know how special they are.

I believe that there is a future for anyone who believes in it. I now know that a chance to work towards the future with my family and my close friends is all I want in my life.

The one good thing I know about life is that when I have everyone around me supporting me, it makes me feel special. I am very proud of what I have done in my life, and should be proud of it. I am delighted with myself. I would never change anything about anyone in my life.

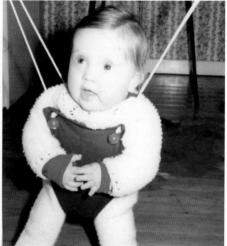
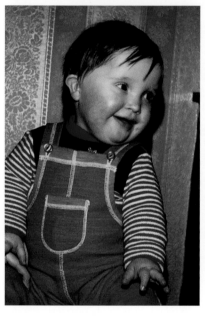

My Family and Me

My family is important to me in many ways. They have given me all the support and all the help that I need. I know how special they are. They have given me something that I never knew I had – the belief that I have talent and ability.

I will tell you about my family. We are very outgoing and we do things together like going away to different places. We are there for each other when we need help.

I believe there is a soulmate for anyone. You have to remember how special your soulmate is to you. My brother Eoin is my soulmate and hero. Myself and my brother go to see matches in pubs around here in Newbridge. We always do that anytime when he is around and when he is not too busy.

My sister Jenny has always been there for me. When I was little she used to boss me because she wanted me to be the best I could be. Sometimes I would get mad at her and then we would fall around the place laughing. I love her very much and always will.

My dad is a Colonel in the Defence Forces and now works in Vienna for the ambassador. Because of his career he is sometimes away from home. I miss him a lot when he is away but I email him and he rings me. He is very special because he brings me to all the matches in Dublin. I always find it easy to talk to my dad. He helps me sort out my problems and plans.

My mother always believed in me and supports me in my dreams and hopes. She knew that I could learn and live my life to the full. She always helped me when I needed her help but encouraged me to be independent. Because of her I can do everything for myself now, and she is proud of me. She has taught me that I should be proud of myself and what I have achieved in my life. I think that is very important.

The Gannons and the Fahys

My parents had two different families back in those days. They were the Gannon family on one side and on the other side we had my mother's family, the Fahys. They all got to know each other. Sometimes they would meet up for a drink and talk about the old times when they were young, and look back at memories that they had together.

In the Gannon family we had Kitty Gannon, who was very special to me. She died on 28 April 2009. My whole family was devastated. She was eighty-three years old. The year before she died, I wrote this about her:

> Kitty does everything for herself and is living her life to the full. If she wants someone to help her, we all help. Let us hope that she will stay with us for as long as possible. She is a wonderful person to be with. We all know that she has lost her brother a few weeks ago. But she is still here and she is amazing and looking well.

Grandad Bill Gannon died in 1983, so I don't really remember him at all. Dad has three brothers: Liam, Paddy and Gerry. Liam has three children: two girls and a boy. Their names are Siobhan, Deirdre and Cathal. Liam works very hard in construction. Their children are in school. His wife Ann works hard as well. They both like Irish dancing. They also do everything and go out to matches and holidays together. They sometimes read books and listen to music and stay together like a family should.

Paddy and Catriona Gannon have two sons, Peter and Stephen. In 2008 Peter got married and we all had a great time in Durrow Castle for the wedding. On the day of the wedding, the weather was bright and sunny, the food was great, and everything went well. Dawn was the bride and looked very well. She was a bit nervous at first because she wanted everything to go well. It did go well, for one and all.

Stephen was the best man. He had a speech to make about Peter on the day of the wedding. He was funny at times, getting the *craic* out of everyone. We all had a great laugh. Stephen did a great job on the speech.

Gerry and Christine have two children: Laura and Sara. They are great fun to be with and can be very funny at times. When we have a party to bring in the New

Year, they come down and bring their instruments. Their parents sing. Everyone sings along with them and helps them out with a song of their choice.

My father has two sisters: Josie and Bee. Josie and Jimmy Lynch have two kids: Orla and Conor. Jimmy is a farmer and Josie is a nurse. The Lynches do everything for themselves and are very lucky to have each other. They also go to matches together and they always have the *craic*. They come to our parties and always look back to what life was like back in those times when they were young.

Bee and Jim Kirby have two kids: James and Catherine. They are great to be with. In the football they support Kerry. James and Catherine are both in school in Dublin. They also go on holidays together. They sometimes go to Mayo. Bee is a nurse and works very hard. She is very outgoing. Jim is a teacher. Catherine and James play music and bring their instruments down to our house for parties.

The other side of the family is my mother's side, the Fahys. When I was very young, I spent a lot of time with my Granddad and Granny Fahy in Kilkenny. Granddad loved the horses and we used to back them in the bookies. We had great fun together. I missed him when he died in 1997. Everyone in my mother's life is important to her and has played a major part in her life, and in mine as well. That is why families should stay together through good and tough times. It is also about looking forward to what the future may hold and to look back on the memories that we have together.

Granny Fahy – or Granny Bridie, as I used to call her – smoked a lot. She was fun to be with. She loved shopping and spoiling me. She died in 1998.

My mother has one sister and three brothers. Her sister Breed lives in Luton, England, so we don't see her very often. She was, and still is, a good sister to my mother. Breed has three children: Wesley, Sara Jane and Kenneth. They all live in England.

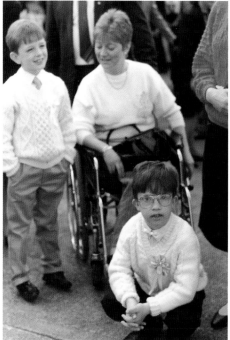

Her brother Liam lives in Kilkenny and is married to Susan. They have three children: Billy, Hazel and Emma. They are great cousins to be with. We have had great times together talking, laughing and having a meal. Billy got married to Lauren in 2010. It was a great party. All the Fahy family got together. The wedding was in Ballycallan church in Kilkenny. Lauren is from America. She looked really well in her wedding dress. She wasn't nervous herself. Liam made a great speech about Billy.

Niall Fahy is married to Cecilla and also lives in Kilkenny. They have two girls – Olivia and Isobel. They are very special to me. The girls are younger than me but are very funny and laugh a lot.

The baby of my mother's family is my Uncle Paddy. Paddy lives in Cashel, Tipperary. Sometimes he supports Kilkenny, where he was born, and sometimes Tipperary, where he lives. His wife is Caroline and he has four children – Aisling, Rachel, Vanessa and Patrick. The children are much younger then I am. One day Patrick might play hurling for Kilkenny.

And so these are my grandparents, aunts, uncles and cousins. We have had good times together. I am lucky to have them.

School Years

The first school I went to was up in the Curragh. It was called St Ann's School. When I was five I started in Scoil Mhuire National School. I was the only one in the school who had Down syndrome. The classes were a bit big at that time. But we had enough space for the teachers and for all the students. There were helpers who helped me there. My mother helped me with the homework that I had to do. Every night I did all my homework with the help from my mother.

I know that I have Down syndrome but I worked very hard. I was a bit nervous coming into this school. Sometimes I did not know what was going on but the teachers helped and everyone got to know me.

Mrs Nancy Grennan helped to do maths. She used to say: 'There is a computer in your head, use it!' Mrs Egan was my special teacher. She came and worked with me every day until the end of third class.

Then I saw the Patrician Brothers Secondary School. I wanted to get into it because they do a school musical every year. When I finished at Scoil Mhuire I did get into PBS and I was in five of them. I was in *Seven Brides for Seven Brothers* and *Joseph and His*

Amazing Technicolor Dream Coat. Viva Mexico was another one I enjoyed, and *Aisling* was another one.

I was a Roman Soldier in *Jesus Christ Superstar*; my brother Eoin played Judas. He was just the best. The practices were great fun. The director that we had was Chris Ford. We all worked very hard to put this show on. Performing in front of everyone was just wonderful.

It was a great feeling to be part of the shows. I did have the most amazing friends. They got to know me very well and I got to know everyone in that school, and that was great as well. It is very important to me that I learn hard things. I want to understand and know what is happening.

There was more to the PBS than shows. The Patrician Brothers Secondary School is a very big school by the River Liffey. The students are all boys. There were over a hundred students in each year. It was easy enough to find my way around. I just went with it. They gave each of us a timetable and you just followed it. My favourite class was music but I really liked reading *Catcher in the Rye* in English class. I worked with a partner for science experiments.

The teachers at PBS were great and helped me a lot. I wanted to prove that I could work on my own. If I needed any help from the teachers I would ask them to help me. They all did. I knew that I did everything right. I even got to drive the car in transition year. I got my exam results, and they were good and I deserved them. I was given an honour at the end of sixth year.

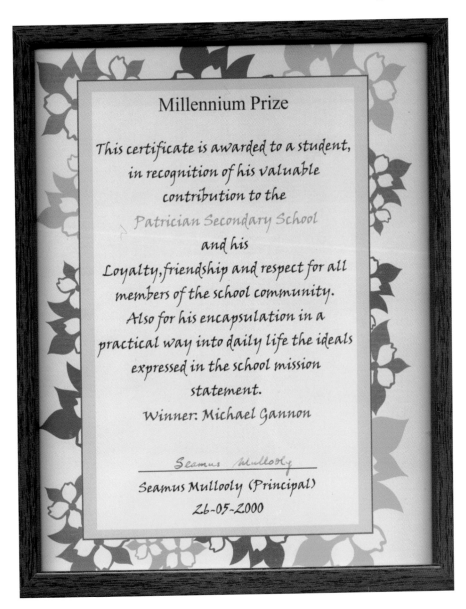

Millennium Prize

This certificate is awarded to a student,
in recognition of his valuable
contribution to the
Patrician Secondary School
and his
Loyalty, friendship and respect for all
members of the school community.
Also for his encapsulation in a
practical way into daily life the ideals
expressed in the school mission
statement.
Winner: Michael Gannon

Seamus Mullooly
Seamus Mullooly (Principal)
26-05-2000

I won the Millennium Award at Graduation. I was very privileged and honoured. This is what the certificate looked like:

The time after leaving PBS was very hard for me. I was sure I wanted to be an actor but I did not know how to get there. I never lost the dream, and my mother helped.

Then the FAS course came up. It was called 'An Introduction to the Arts'. It lasted for one school year. I did some work with Terry Moore in the Riverbank Arts Centre in Newbridge. I did front of house and some ushering. It was a start and I met loads of friends.

Then I applied and got into the VTOS Programme. You can't believe how happy this made me. The modules I took were: Computers, ECDL (European

Computer Driving Licence); Community and Street Theatre; Performance Craft; Communications Skills and Personal Development.

When I was in VTOS, I made the most amazing friends. They helped me all the way to get through everything that I needed to do to complete my studies. Ann Mekitarian was my drama coach and guided me. The results that I got were good. I was happy. I worked very hard. I had great time and would love to go back.

In VTOS we put on a few plays. They were great to do. We all worked very hard on these plays. We did have some laughs on the way but most of all we had to practise the plays together. That was the most important thing we had to do. Most of the plays were funny at times.

This was a good experience for me because I felt that I had something to do. I was learning new things. I was with good people. My family supported me throughout my stay in VTOS. That felt great. They also felt very proud of what I have done.

I made up a poem about my stay in VTOS when I was there. I hope I can remember the poem. I want to share it with you. I want you to read it and see if you like it. The poem is called 'Tribute to VTOS'.

Tribute to VTOS

Looking back is hard to do
Being here is something new
Every room I see a face
Telling me that this is the right place.

Dreams are real and make them true
I am here and so are you
You make my day a perfect day
Students and tutors, my friends today
Something easy, something hard
Something new that I have found.
Emotions run high,

There is tension all around.
My heart will not stop,
That's what I have found.
I come to learn and nothing else
Having tutors to teach is the best
You touch my heart with gold.

Then I had to move on and do other things. I know this is hard, but sometimes I have to look forward in my own life. Saying goodbye is very emotional for me. When I look back on those days in my life I do miss them one and all.

Hobbies

Well, what can I tell about myself and my hobbies? Let me see. How can I start? I am interested in reading books, listening to music, and playing my bodhrán. I am also an actor. I like setting up an office space for myself. I am often busy working on my own. I also like to write poems, and some day I want to make up plays for the different groups that I am involved in.

I am a good organiser and work very hard in what I do. I keep very busy every day. I am also a member of my local gym. The gym is just across the road from me. I go over there five days a week unless I am too busy. I have a timetable for

exercise. It is all easy enough and it keeps me fit. I am very active as well. I always do everything for myself and try to look well.

Another hobby that I really like to do is to write poems. In a poem I can express how I feel about anything I want to do in my own life. A poem can also express my ups and downs and how I feel about my own childhood and my family life. A poem can also express all of those feelings that we have for each other.

My other big hobby has been writing this book. I have worked on it on my

own when no one was around. It kept me busy during the day. Well, at least I was doing something for myself. As I have already said, my goal was to get this book done.

Another of my hobbies is listening to music. When I listen to music it can be very relaxing, especially when I work really hard with no one around. My favourite kind of music is country and western. Some singers I like are Garth Brooks, Shania Twain and Eoin Gannon. Eoin is my brother and he is a singer and songwriter. I remember when he used to bring his guitar up to his room and sing his heart out. I tell him that he is nearly the best singer that I know. He is a great singer, but he is not as good as me. I am a good singer, you know. My family thinks that I am not. I just prove them wrong with my singing ability (choke, choke).

I play the bodhrán. I got my bodhrán for my birthday a few years ago from all my relations. It is kind of a drum. You hold the bodhrán in your left hand and beat the rhythm with a stick in your left hand. It takes a lot of practice. I always play at family parties when everyone is around, especially at New Year's. Sometimes my parents do Irish dancing to our music. Jenny sings as well.

A few years ago I was given a digital camera for my birthday. I enjoy taking pictures of some places around and when I go on trips. Some of my photos are really cool. This is one that I took of the River Liffey near where I live.

My hobbies are important to me. I am never bored.

Holidays

I went on my own to the French retreat at Jean Vanier's. I went there three times with my friends David and Emily. We met up with other people from around Ireland in Dublin airport. What do you think we did over there? Well, I can tell you.

First we got our keys and went into our different rooms just to settle in. We got our things ready and then we had our food. Then we had evening prayer. Then we divided into sharing groups. Jean Vanier encouraged us to share our lives with each other - the things that make us happy and sad – our plans, fears and dreams.

Sometimes we had Mass as well. Sometimes I served Mass. We often went for walks together. We had a few singing sessions and a few parties in our rooms. We

enjoyed it all. We got to know each other a bit more and we all loved it. We became very close friends. The retreats have been some of the best holidays that I have had.

Since I was a member of the YCS choir in the Dominican Church I have gone to Knockadoon, Cork, during August just to have some time with friends on

my own away from my family. I go with a bunch of others. We take the train from Newbridge to Cork, then a bus to Knockadoon. I love it. Knockadoon is a camp where you go to learn church music.

At Knockadoon we take part in music tutorials. The team help us play our instruments better. The tutors are there to give us a hand. We listen to different types of music. We do Mass and a concert in the village on the Saturday night. The Mass is great because everybody sings and the leaders play guitars, bongos and other instruments. After Mass we have a bonfire night at the camp. In Knockadoon everybody has to pitch in and do a job. There is a rota. We take turns doing different jobs. I like cleaning tables after meals. It is a good way to get to know other people.

On some of our family holidays we have gone to Spain. We go over there to have our own holiday and to be together. We always have a great time. The last time we went out to the beach and my mother and father started dancing on the beach.

It was an amazing performance – *strictly* amazing! They were so funny together. I fell about laughing so much that I could not stop myself. We must go back there soon.

We had a holiday in Brussels when my father worked there. My mother, Jenny, Eoin and I went over to see him. We had a great time but dad worked very hard while the rest of us went sightseeing. We saw different things that we liked to see and sometimes we went shopping. We got ourselves something to wear. We all got new clothes over there.

My father was re-located to Vienna, Austria, in August 2009 for two and half years. In 2010 we all flew to Vienna to join him after Christmas. We nearly missed the trip because there was so much snow in Dublin and the airports kept closing. But we made it. I did not know that the airport was such a good place for shopping. In Vienna we went sightseeing and took photos.

The high point for me was going with my dad to an ice hockey match between Vienna Capitals and Anderlecht. I loved the game. I took photos. The stadium was massive. The motto of the Vienna Capitals is 'Fire on Ice'. Vienna won and I was delighted. I had a great time with my father.

Sports

I am a sports fan. I follow Manchester United in football. For one of my birthdays we all went over to see the team play at Old Trafford and had a great time. I would love to go back there again. I am into international soccer and support my Irish team. Let us hope that we can do very well and have a good manager. Let us hope we win more games.

I am also a hurling man. I follow Kilkenny and I am proud of it. During 2006-2009 Kilkenny were the champions and won the Liam McCarthy Cup four times in a row. Every time they won my family and I went down to Kilkenny to see and cheer the team's homecoming. I was very proud to be from Kilkenny.

I also love rugby. In 2009 the Irish rugby team won the RBS Six Nations Grand Slam. It had been sixty-one years since we had won the Grand Slam. The same day Bernard Dunne won the world championship in boxing. This was the best week for Irish sport. We were proud to be Irish, and why not? This was just wonderful, and a great feeling to have in our country. I hope we can do it again in years to come.

Acting Career

A long time ago I decided that I wanted to be an actor. I was in Betty Ann Norton's School of Acting. I was a teacher in a play. Since then I have loved being on stage. Sometimes even now I get nervous before I go on the stage but I leave my nerves behind and keep going and do my best.

After that I was getting more interested in drama so I continued on with it. I felt I had more shows to come and more parts as well. One day I read this in a small book:

There is always one moment in childhood
when the door opens and lets in the future.

I used to say this to myself and it meant something very important to me. This is when I started to believe in myself as an actor.

School plays came next and they were spectacular. Then I was a member of the Kildare Youth Theatre and loved being part of it. It was all about drama and getting more involved with all my friends. All of them were just wonderful to be with. We all got to know everyone and got parts in plays. I really liked doing this because I needed acting experience.

The KYT group had an exchange weekend in Edinburgh with the West Lothian Youth Theatre. We travelled by plane on Friday and we stayed in a hostel. There were fifteen in our group and we had prepared a drama piece to do. It was about the experience of being bullied. Everyone had a part to play.

At the beginning everyone was silent and in different groups. In each group

there was one person who was being bullied. Slowly people began moving. It was like a Mexican wave, one group copying another. Then the music began. Little by little the groups included the outsiders and they all supported each other with friendship. Everyone thought it was very good.

This is why I think drama is very good for self-development. It gives a chance to experience feelings and find ways to solve problems. We all in KYT had a great time together and learned a lot.

In 2008 the Newbridge Pantomime Group presented *Beauty and the Beast*. The Newbridge Musical Society did *42nd Street*. I was involved with both of the shows and all the shows since then. It was great and I got my chance to do the thing that I like to do. Performing in front of my family and friends is the best experience that anyone could have and I was very honoured to do this. I get a wonderful feeling on stage. It is the greatest buzz I have ever had.

Everything about doing the shows is wonderful. I love the rehearsals. Show time is magic. The costumes, music, make-up, standing ovations! Being part of the group makes it even better for me. I am a part of it.

I am well known as an actor to my friends. The people I know have come to see all the pantomimes and all the musicals I have been in. They have given me huge support. It is a great feeling to have my family and friends in the audience because they see my ability. I get the chance to see them after the show and they celebrate with me. I am getting my chance now to continue my acting career thanks to everyone who gave me a chance.

My Dream Job

My job working for RTÉ as TV reporter on *The Afternoon Show* is a dream job. I could not believe it when I was told I got the job. I was in shock and everyone was delighted for me.

Just before I got this job I was on the TV3 morning programme, *Ireland AM*, talking to the presenters about the World Down Syndrome Congress in Dublin. Grainne Murphy was with me on the programme. They were asking me questions about myself and my work. Soon afterwards I met someone from RTÉ. They interviewed me for this role as a TV reporter with a unique view. They wanted someone to give reports on different topics.

So I got my chance to work on RTÉ. The people from RTÉ are very supportive to me and help me. My family help me with the reports that I have to do for this job. They

help me get my reports done before I go on *The Afternoon Show*. I am delighted to work with them now and also they are delighted with me and my reports. So far my reports have been about interesting topics. Some were on the *Titanic* show at Citywest, Dublin pantomimes and Astronomy Ireland. I have interviewed some members of the Irish rugby team and Brian Cody, the Kilkenny hurling manager.

Not so long ago I was sent to interview the famous twin-duo Jedward in the Liffey Studios in Dublin. They were rehearsing for their pantomime Cinderella. I danced with them while we sang 'Under Pressure Ice Ice Baby'. It was an amazing interview. John and Edward are real professionals. Really cool.

Being a TV reporter is a good job because I enjoy meeting new people. I like the challenge of being on time for the show to start. To get to RTÉ I take the 12:26 train from Newbridge to Heuston Station in Dublin and then take a

taxi to the TV station. I have to be there at 2:30. I do not want to be late. I have always been on time.

When I get to RTÉ the first thing I do is give my name to the woman at the desk and then I go to the green room. I have my lunch, go to make-up, and then the show begins. There are other people in the green room who will also be in the programme. I get to meet them and talk to them. The best thing is when I go on. I am not nervous. It is a great feeling to have.

World Down Syndrome Congress

The 10th World Down Syndrome Congress was held in Dublin in August 2009 at DCU college. Fifty-two Irish people with Down syndrome were chosen as ambassadors for the Congress. Five training centers were set up around the country where ambassadors learned how to welcome guests. All of us had different jobs to do. Some worked on the information desk. Others introduced speakers.

The day before the Congress opened, the first ever Synod of People with Down Syndrome took place. The Synod was held in the Royal Hospital Kilmainham. We talked about employment and living in the community. David Hingsburger helped us. Only people who had Down syndrome were eligible to speak. Some of the delegates got the chance to speak up for themselves. Everyone did really well.

We all should be proud of what we said. All through the Congress we worked

very hard. We stayed on the campus in student apartments. It was a good chance to be with my friends. There was a full programme of interest to us. Sometimes we had lots of fun in the workshops. Two of the workshops I thought were cool were 'Exploring Identity Through Drama and Citizenship' and 'Playing Your Part in Society'. We also had a film-making workshop and different experts talking about fitness and beauty secrets.

Also, as part of the Congress, a large group of us performed with Cathy O'Kennedy's dance troupe, Counterbalance. We had two performances that were massive. The dance programme was called the Echoes Project because the groups of dancers came from all over Ireland. It had another meaning also because we kept copying and responding to each other in the dances.

I have always wanted to dance because it is a good way to express myself. Before Counterbalance I did not get a chance to do so. Now this was just magic. At the end of the performances we all felt wonderful. We had practised hard and were very good. Our work had paid off.

At the end of the Congress we had prizes for all the leaders who had helped us all the way. All the ambassadors were very proud of the leaders. We appreciated their support and all their laughter. We danced a lot. All the leaders had a great time as well. We hope we can go to South Africa in 2012 for the next Congress if we earn the money. We had such a good time that I might become a conference junkie. This is a poem I wrote about the DS World Congress, Dublin, August 2009.

Welcome to the World Congress

The World Down Syndrome Congress
has come to Ireland.
We, the host nation, are proud to be Irish.
We welcome you one and all.
We hope you have a great time here -
Share lots of good experiences,
And make new friends with one and all.
We come together to celebrate
with friends we have made one and true.
We will laugh and have fun together
share the gifts and talents we have.

We know the gift of life is special
Being here makes our dreams come true.
Dreams are real.
We make them true in the special times we spend together.
Life is a challenge
But we're not afraid
We face our goals honestly, strongly, hopefully.

Drama, Music, Dance,
All the leaders behind us
We discover talents
We did not know we had.
With love and happiness, the best gifts of all
That is what we treasure
So thank you to one and all
Up the Irish from me to you
Let's party on now.

Brussels

I was lucky enough to take part in the European Programme - My Opinion My Vote (MOTE). The first meeting we had together was in Brussels. The Irish team who travelled to Brussels for this programme were: Cathy Soden from Dublin, Orla Hannon from Clare, John Sweetnam from Cork, Declan Murphy from Waterford, David Clarke from Louth and myself, Michael Gannon from Kildare. We travelled on Wednesday 28 January by plane from Dublin to Brussels.

When we arrived we met Mairead McGuinness, an Irish member of the European Parliament. She talked to us for a few minutes and we had our photos taken with her. We had just a few minutes with her because we had to do a presentation on living with a disability in our country. We needed to tell others about Ireland. There were six other countries at the course. We heard about Malta, Spain, Denmark, Italy and Hungary too.

We visited the European Parliament and the European Commission. As part of our training in Cork before we had left, Mary Murphy at UCC had told us about these two places. We bought our own lunch at the canteen in the Parliament. It was packed with people who work for the Parliament and the Commission. Later we learned about voting and it was fun. I have already voted in our Irish elections.

We talked about different countries in the European Union. We learned about the European anthem and the flags from the different countries. Each night we went for dinner with the people from other countries. The team leaders helped us understand what the people were saying who didn't speak English.

On the last day we had a training session about the issues that affect our lives. The topics were employment, equal rights, citizenship, education and independent living. The last afternoon we travelled by train to Bruges. We went shopping and had lunch. We bought lots of Belgian chocolates for our families. The chocolates were made in many shapes, some were even shaped like women's boobs. They were very funny but I did not buy them. We had a great time.

I believe this programme was very important because people who happen to have a disability have opinions and votes. We need to be heard and we must use our right to vote. We need to stand up for ourselves.

Citizenship is important because we all make choices and must be responsible. We all have a right to express our opinions. We need to know how to be good citizens. We also need to stand up for ourselves. We need to be heard. Citizens have duties, rights and privileges. We all have equal rights and we all should believe in them. It is very important that everyone be open-minded and respectful of others. It is good to listen to each other.

Budapest

The second phase of the MOTE programme was in Budapest, Hungary. Our Team Ireland had to do another presentation on living with a disability in Ireland. Other countries had to make presentations on the same topic.

I learned that in Hungary if you have a disability you cannot vote in the elections because their rights have been taken away. They have been interdicted by the court. A guardian is appointed for them. George, who was from Hungary, was very upset because he couldn't get married. He had no disability allowance and he couldn't vote. A guardian was appointed for him and nobody spoke to him about it or asked his permission.

We also went to the Hungarian Parliament, where we met the politicians. Monique from Italy told them about her life and the MOTE programme. George from Hungary told them about his rights having been taken away because he

had been interdicted by the courts. The leaders spoke about the MOTE programme and asked the politicians to think about the difficult situation in Hungary for people with disability.

Delegates to the MOTE programme visited the Down Foundation Centre in

Budapest. Here I learned that in Hungary at fourteen years of age there is no school allowed if you have a disability. So you have to stay at home with your parents or go into a centre and work there. They were making key-rings and jewellery. This would not by my kind of thing to do every day. I would not like to work there myself.

We also went to the Ombudsman's office. This is the office you go to if you have a complaint about your rights. We spoke about the rights of people with disability in Hungary. They said they are trying to change the situation for people like George.

Rome

The third and final trip of the MOTE programme was to Rome. We all had a great time in Rome. We went sightseeing and saw different places. We also had Holy Mass on Sunday in a very old church. We went to late-morning Mass. The church was cold but the music was very beautiful and relaxing. There was a fantastic choir singing. Most of the people from other countries slept in and did not go. The Mass went on for a very long time but it was worth getting up for.

We visited the Italian Parliament and went on the tour around the building and saw different paintings in different rooms. We went out to dinner and tasted the Italian food in different restaurants. Some of us lads had Italian beer. It was quite good. The girls would not taste the beer. They said they did not like it. Everyone drank responsibly. We all had a great time and got to know each other well.

As part of the MOTE programme we visited five different group homes where some people with Down syndrome live. They showed us around their place and their rooms as well. They live independently and it was great to see them.

We went to the Parliament to practise for the talk show: *I Think, I Choose, I Am*. One delegate from each country made a speech. We had Orla Hannon representing Ireland. She did very well. Team Ireland were very proud of her.

One of the best highlights of my stay in Rome was going from the hotel to the Italian Parliament on Paola's motorbike. She took David, Declan and myself in turns on the back of her huge noisy bike. We really flew through the traffic. She was brilliant!

The last Wednesday, when we had the evaluation in Rome, everyone came together and said goodbye. I was very emotional and sad. This was our last day together for the MOTE programme. We had shared so much. That had been very important.

When we got back we gave a presentation to members of the Irish Parliament, the Dáil. We told them that it was very important that they listen to the opinion of people who happen to have a disability. It is My Opinion, My Vote. We also spoke to President Mary McAleese. She listened carefully to what we had to say. This is a photo of us on duty – and off duty.

Memories

I remember most of my childhood. I have good memories of when I was small. I think I can recall a memory of myself and my granddad. We used to back horses in Kilkenny. That is one of my favourite memories of him. I will always remember Kitty. She had a smile that touched many people's hearts.

I remember when I was very young the whole family went down to Wicklow. We had some laughs on the way down there. The weather was very sunny and warm as well. We had great times together.

When I was ten my father did a course in Leavenworth, Kansas. He was sent there by the Irish Defence Forces. The whole family went to the States for a year. We all had a great time over there and the weather was sunny and hot. We had a car and drove all over the States. Sometimes we stopped for a few days. Like true Americans we always had something to eat.

As we travelled we played a game called States and Capitals. We had to remember all fifty states and their capital cities. My father and Eoin won most of the time. We really did have fun with this game when we were travelling. This game was the best ever. There were times when we were travelling about that I could not stop laughing because we were having such a good time going everywhere and seeing new things.

I went to Xavier Catholic School in Leavenworth. Sister Regina Maria took me for special help. She taught me to pronounce my 'th' sound. She was fun, and very good to me, and helped me a lot. Mrs Myers was my teacher. I was the only one who had Down syndrome in the school but that was not a problem.

I am a big fan of country and western music. The whole family went to see the Grand Ole Opry theatre. There was a concert in Nashville and we went to see it. This was a great experience for me because I am a big fan. I have some CDs of country music.

I always have memories – good, bad and funny ones. Talking about them helps me think about the past, present and future. We always do it every year at New Year's day and look forward to what the future may hold. Life can be hard at times and looking back can be a very hard thing to do. But you have to move on and do better things that you can look back on later. Life can be good.

Dreams

I will tell you about my dreams. One dream would be to appear on *Strictly Come Dancing*. It would be great to learn the dances and it would be a challenge for me. Dancing is one of my interests. I can now dance well. It would be brilliant to appear on this programme. But I do not think this will happen.

Another dream has been to get this book done. Then I could get ready for the launch of my book. I could get my invitations out to all my friends. It will be a great celebration. I have been writing this book for a long while now and I am now making good progress.

I wanted to write this book because I want people to know who I am and how I cope with having Down syndrome. Writing this book was hard for me because I hate having Down syndrome, but I do. But deep down in my heart I don't have Down syndrome.

I hope I will do a documentary about this book because this is something important for me. I have never written a film before so this is my chance to do something new for myself. I will have to learn a lot of new techniques. It will be interesting to know how people will react to this film. I hope they will react to it in a positive way. I hope they will enjoy it.

I have been thinking about some music for the documentary. The songs I have in my mind are 'You Raise Me Up', 'Two Sides to Every Story' and 'You've Got a Friend'. The reason why I have chosen these songs is because I do like listening to them and each of them explains how I feel about my life.

If you are reading this at least one of my dreams has come true. My next dream would be to celebrate the book launch with my friends and family. See you there!

Moving On

Moving on for me is very important. I have so many things going on at the moment. I have got a place in Maynooth doing Media Studies and this will help me to learn different skills.

When I heard that I got a place in NUI Maynooth doing Media Studies I was over the moon. My family and friends were delighted for me. Now at least I have found something that I really like doing. Now I need to do all the hard work by studying.

This course will help me with the work I do in RTE. I am delighted that I am back this season to do more reports.

My father who was serving in Vienna will be officially retiring in February 2012. And I will be delighted to see him home for good this time. My whole family and myself will have lot of celebrating when he gets home.

In August 2012 Eoin and Colleen will be married. I will be his best man. I will be looking forward to the wedding next year.

Photograph by Deasy Photographic

Acknowledgements

I would like to thank you all for what you have done for me throughout my life. I would first like to mention my family. You have made me the happiest man alive. I am still your son and that means a lot to me. I know I am not perfect but I am still here. Where would I have been without you? This book is all about the ups and downs and good times we have had together. I feel that I am very lucky to have such a great family who have supported me all the way. My parents are proud of me, and should be.

All I ever wanted to do was to act on the stage. I have been given the chance to do what I do best. I want to thank the people who gave me a chance to act. I wanted to share my acting skills. Now I perform on stage with my friends. That is all I want – to perform.

My editor, Mercedes Egan, is someone who helped me a lot with this book. Without her this book would not have happened. I have known her twenty-five years now and would like to say thank you. You have been my good friend. I am very proud of you and what you have done in your life. You have had a major impact on me over those twenty-five years, so thank you.

My last word is to all the readers of my book. I want to say to you, believe in yourself and in the abilities of everyone around you, even if they have Down syndrome.

Editor's Afterword

Several years ago Michael approached me about writing a book about his life. I casually agreed that this was a good idea. Then a notebook appeared, then another notebook, and another, then a title, another title, a table of contents (without the contents), a table of contents (with contents), and then the laptop. I knew then that there was an unstoppable force to be reckoned with and gave in to the plan.

In each of these early stages, Michael had given long and careful consideration to the implications of writing his story. He had thought of the requirements and had elected to follow his dream. He had filled in his table of contents and knew where he wanted to go, even though sometimes we took the scenic route. It has been a wonderful journey working with my author.

From nearly the beginning Michael had chosen, and was totally committed to, the title *What You See Is What You Get*. I believe he chose this title as a commitment

to telling the truth about his life. I am sure that it held other significance for him, but we will let him tell us about that some day. So having lived with this title as his own for a long time, you can imagine his chagrin to walk into a bookstore before Christmas 2010 and see Sir Alan Sugar's biography *What*

You See Is What You Get! Devastation. Down but never out, a new title emerged: *Straight Up, No Sugar*. Again, nothing but the real, the deeply believed, the truth.

I think Michael would agree when I observe that people who experience disability have an important life story and often wish to tell it. Their stories are intuitive, funny and courageous. Their stories contain many messages and insights that everyone should know. However, their work is sometimes criticised as having been assisted to an extent which makes it not their own work.

In my editorial role I have used the following guidelines and disciplines:

- Author chooses topic and composes draft.
- Author and editor edit text together.
- Author has control of laptop.
- Editor can suggest deletions – usually repetitions.
- Editor can suggest order and arrangement of content.
- Editor can suggest topics that the author may not have covered.
- Editor can ask questions regarding text, remember author's reply and repeat it so that author may include it in text.
- Spelling corrections and punctuation can be suggested by editor or word-processor programme.
- Author has final say.

It has been a unique pleasure to have supported Michael in his challenge to himself to write this book. All motivation to do so came from him. There were times when it was difficult for Michael to express his deep feelings and find words to speak what was in his heart, but he never evaded the challenge.

Michael, warmest congratulations on a fine book.

Mercedes Egan PhD, 6 February 2011